Apostle Peter Speaks from Heaven:

A Divine Revelation

Matthew Robert Payne

This book is copyrighted by Matthew Robert Payne. Copyright © 2018. All rights reserved.

Any part of this book can be photocopied, stored, or shared with anyone for the purpose of encouraging people as long as you properly credit the author. You are free to quote this book, use whole chapters of this book on blog posts, or use this book to spread the message of Jesus with credit to the author. No further consent from the author is required of you.

Please visit http://personal-prophecy-today.com to sow into Matthew's writing ministry, to request a personal prophecy or life coaching, or to contact him.

Cover designed by akira007 at fiverr.com.

Edited by Lisa Thompson at www.writebylisa.com You can email Lisa at writebylisa@gmail.com for your editing needs.

All scripture is taken from the New King James Version. Copyright © 1982 by Thomas Nelson, Inc. Used by permission. All rights reserved.

The opinions expressed by the author are not necessarily those of Christian Book Publishing USA.

Published by Christian Book Publishing USA.

Christian Book Publishing USA is committed to excellence in the publishing industry. Book design Copyright © 2018 by Christian Book Publishing USA. All rights reserved.

Paperback: 978-1-68411-509-9

Hardcover: 978-1-68411-510-5

Dedication

I want to dedicate this book to my friend, Mitchell Evans. He is a good friend of mine and my pastor. He treats me well and has loved me through many different circumstances for the past six years. It's important to have people in your life that love you for who you are and accept you in the process of your spiritual growth. Mitchell has been that type of friend to me.

I want to also dedicate this book to Robyn Evans, Mitchell's wife. She is a friend with plenty of wonderful things to say to me and encourage me. Mitchell and Robin have been very loyal to me and have always been a great support in all things. I thank them for their faithful friendship.

Acknowledgements

I want to thank my mother and father for all the love that they have given me. I want to thank Jesus, the Father, and the Holy Spirit for being part of my life and for leading me. I want to thank all of my friends, including Andrea, Lisa, and Mary, who love and support me.

I want to thank Bill Vincent from Christian Book Publishing USA for publishing my book and Lisa Thompson for editing my books. If you need an editor, contact her at writebylisa@gmail.com for more information. I also want to thank the people who have sown into my ministry who make it possible for me to publish this book.

I want to thank you, the reader, for deciding to buy this book and for believing in me enough to read it. I hope that you have been blessed by some of my books already. If this is the first book of mine that you have read, I hope that this book will encourage you to read more of my books.

I want to especially thank the Lonis family who donated money for the production of this book right when I needed the funds.

Table of Contents

Dedication 3

Acknowledgements 4

Matthew's Question 7

    Question 1. How do you feel about being here today, Peter? 7

Rebecca's Questions 10

    Question 2. How did the coming of the Holy Spirit at Pentecost change you? 10

    Question 3. How did Jesus use your weaknesses? 12

    Question 4. You walked on water and started sinking. What was that like? 15

    Question 5. How did you feel when Jesus rebuked you? 18

Matthew's Questions 21

    Question 6. What do you like about heaven? 21

    Question 7. What is Jesus like in heaven? 26

    Question 8. What must a person do to go to heaven? 28

Jeff's Questions 31

    Question 9. What was your daily walk with Jesus like? How could you put this into words for us who are seeking God's kingdom, God, Jesus, and the Holy Spirit? 31

        A. What was your walk with Jesus like on earth? 31

        B. How was your walk with Jesus after he left? 34

    Question 10. Can you describe the love of God and Jesus for his children? 37

Question 11. When you experienced your heart break after denying Jesus three times, what change in insight did you have? How did your feelings change? What battles did you face? Did you know God would forgive you?... 39

Question 12. How will I know when I talk to Jesus versus talking to the Father and not show any disrespect to either? 42

Question 13. What is the best advice you can give in order to grow intimate with Jesus, God, and the Holy Spirit? 45

Question 14. Where and how do I learn to draw closer to the Trinity in order to hear their voices distinctly and know that I'm doing God's will? I want to be in sync with them like Jesus was with God. 47

Question 15. How do I seek God with all my heart? What does that mean?.. 50

Question 16. If I surrender my all to God, does that mean I will lose my wife, family, and job to do his will?... 53

Matthew's Question 56

Question 17. Do you have any final thoughts? 56

I'd love to hear from you... 58

How to Sponsor a Book Project... 60

Other Books by Matthew Robert Payne 62

About Matthew Robert Payne 65

MATTHEW'S QUESTION

Question 1. How do you feel about being here today, Peter?

It's really exciting to be here. It's wonderful to be in your house to come and visit you. It's going to be very interesting to be here, answer your questions, and answer the questions of your friends, Rebecca and Jeff, who came up with most of the questions.

It was very delightful of you to put out the questions to your friends. It was a nice thing to do. It will be good for Rebecca and Jeff to be able to read this book and see their questions answered by me.

This time, you have questions that you don't know the answer to in a book. Many times when you interview the saints, you usually know the answers to the questions that you ask. In a lot of instances, you have a good idea of what the answers are.

Today, you're faced with some questions that you couldn't possibly make up clear answers for. You're faced with having to totally rely on me and on what I have to say. In that way, it's interesting to be here, to be able to talk to you, and to be able to share my life with you.

I'm aware of the questions not only because you have them typed on a Microsoft Word document, but I had the questions before me in heaven, and I knew what I was going to speak on before Jeff and Rebecca even posed the questions and before you composed the sheet with the final questions.

I really am happy to be here. It's a real privilege to be invited down here to speak to the people on earth. Of course, your book won't be read by tens of thousands of people. You're not a bestselling author with millions of people who read your books, but the book is for the individuals who are interested enough to buy it.

I must say that I like the cover for the book. It's a great cover. I'm very happy with it. It seems a little mystical and a little Catholic. I'm really pleased with that.

I'd like to consider myself a little mystical. I'd like to consider myself a bit of a sage when it comes to the wisdom of God.

I'm very impressed with the fact that you've persevered with writing this book. You've had some attacks over this book almost to the point of writing to Rebecca and Jeff and telling them that you're going to make up your own questions. Their questions seemed too hard. You normally approach a new project with happiness and glee.

Whenever your schedule clears up, you start another book. Your fears and worries about this book were evident, resulting in a delay in recording this book. So you wisely waited until you felt the compulsion and the unction to actually go ahead and do the book.

I recognize that there were fears and trepidation about this book. I'm so pleased to be in your living room, sitting down and chomping on an apple. You can almost see me sitting here, chomping on an apple, dictating this book to your spirit, spirit to spirit so that you can record what I have to say.

I'm overjoyed to know you, Matthew. I watch your life in heaven. I watch everything you do. I'm very well versed in understanding your past, and I have a good understanding of your future. In heaven, they have movie screens where they show scenes or a movie of a saint's life, their past, and their future. Saints watch those screens and understand what you're doing and what you will achieve on earth.

I understand you now. I understand your struggles, your worries about fitness, and some of the things that are competing for your attention that are getting you down a little. I understand the struggle that you have and some of the troubles that you're facing at the moment. I want you to know that I have a good idea of what you're going through, and I have an understanding nature when it comes to those things.

It's a pleasure to be here, to sit down in your living room, and prepare myself to answer the questions that you have that have been prepared for you by other people for you to ask. You have three questions in the middle, questions six, seven, and eight designed by you. You have asked many saints question six. I look forward to speaking, and we'll just go to question two.

Rebecca's Questions

Question 2. How did the coming of the Holy Spirit at Pentecost change you?

Many people who live in charismatic and Pentecostal circles know what Pentecost is. When you are baptized in the Holy Spirit, you receive an increased empowerment from the Holy Spirit to deal with sin and conquer it in your life. Many times, people receive the gift of tongues, and they have an extra empowerment from the Holy Spirit to facilitate being an effective witness for Christ. Additional gifts from the Holy Spirit are also activated in their lives.

I like to explain that a little differently and perhaps the readers or listeners on Audible can capture what I'm saying. Certain brands of cars can travel on the road, are made for the road, and are made for normal driving, but they have cousins that are super charged with bigger engines or more highly developed engines that they use at race tracks.

The racing companies have those cars at the race tracks to race professionally. When the cars perform really well and win the races, it increases the prestige of that particular car, that model of car. It's supposed to lead to an increase in sales of the traditional car that drives on the roads that's available for the average person to purchase.

The Holy Spirit is like that super-charged car. Not everyone who lives a typical Christian life has received the baptism of the Holy Spirit. A lot of people in traditional churches, who probably wouldn't be listening to or reading this book, have the Holy Spirit in their lives. They're like a normal car on a freeway, but someone who is baptized in the Holy Spirit has that extra spark in their engine, has that extra capacity in their engine to perform really well.

Of course, the high-performing car with the high-performance engine could probably drive on a normal road, but they're usually constrained by the government to travel on race tracks and be carried on a trailer on the back of a car until they get to a race track where they can go full speed.

The Holy Spirit gave me a supercharge. You all remember how I preached at Pentecost, and the anointing, the power of God, came on me and supercharged me. I'm not sure if you've ever listened to certain speakers, but certain speakers have an anointing on their voice. It makes them more relatable, more understandable, and a lot more interesting to listen to.

When someone sings with a normal voice, that can be fine, and you can listen to it. But when God has anointed a voice, it just has a special sound to it. It has a special resonance that stands out; it really attracts your attention and takes you somewhere in the Holy Spirit. It gives you a spiritual experience.

You can have a singer with a normal voice who doesn't really carry and lead you into a place of ecstasy when you're listening to them sing. On the other hand, you can have someone with an anointing of the Holy Spirit on their voice, which actually captures you, takes you to another place, and encourages you to feel the presence of God come upon you because of the way that they worship.

I was super charged like that car. I could operate and go on a normal road. I could mix with normal people, be down to earth, and easy to relate to.

But when I spoke, when I was in a public place, the anointing of the Lord came upon my voice. It made what I said captivating and interesting to listen to. The Holy Spirit worked effectively through my voice to bring conviction to people as I was preaching. It directed the people and led them to a logical conclusion that the Holy Spirit had orchestrated.

The Holy Spirit always has an agenda, a message, and a reason why he has you speak. That agenda is fulfilled through the anointing on your voice. The Holy Spirit not only changed the way I did things, he took away some of my fear and trepidation. He gave me boldness and power. I spoke with authority.

Matthew 7:28 says that the Pharisees and the leaders were amazed, and the people were astonished at Jesus because of the authority that he spoke with. Having the Holy Spirit come at Pentecost gave my voice this rich resonance. It gave my voice this authority. It demanded attention so that my voice stood out and was projected for all to hear.

My personal life was changed. The way I conducted myself was changed. The anointing on my voice and the way I carried a message for God was changed also, which all resulted in more people being saved and wanting to come into the kingdom.

Question 3. How did Jesus use your weaknesses?

I'd like to say that I didn't have any weaknesses. I like to put it on record that I was the perfect disciple, and I didn't have any weaknesses. Ha ha! But people who've listened to sermons throughout the years and listened to what people have had to say about me will probably say that I was quick to speak. When Jesus rebuked me and said, "Get behind me, Satan," this was clear to see. (See Matthew 16:33.) On other occasions, I also proved that I did not put much thought into what I spoke out about and didn't really think too much on my feet.

How did Jesus use that weakness? Well, I like to say that it isn't really a weakness to have curiosity although some people might see it as a weakness. People in a classroom who see a person constantly asking questions might think that the person's stupid. They might think that the person is misbehaving in the class, asking so many questions. They might think that the person is silly. But to a person who is gifted to teach, a person with an insatiable appetite for the things of God, it seems only natural to step out and ask questions when questions come to mind.

Many people sit in a classroom or in a lecture, and questions come to mind, but they don't have the courage or the boldness to raise their hand and ask the question. This is usually because they're embarrassed about what the other people in the lecture hall will say about them and think of their question.

I wasn't afraid of Jesus or of people. I lived my whole life asking questions and asking people to go into detail and give me the root of what they were talking about. I wanted to know the nitty-gritty. I wanted to know everything about everything. I wanted to know more than the actual speaker. I wanted the speaker to find relevant and helpful information on the subject that they were teaching on.

I wanted to push the lecturer. I wanted to push the speaker to give me information that they didn't ordinarily give in a lecture and what they were speaking about. I have this unbelievable mind that loves details.

If people consider that a weakness, I never corrected that. In fact, when the Holy Spirit came at Pentecost, it only activated my mind like that super-charged car I talked about. It put my mind in overdrive. I had a whole lot more communication with the Holy Spirit. Today, modern science would diagnose someone like this with ADHD.

I spoke without thinking, and I continued to speak without thinking. A prominent politician in America at the moment seems to speak without thinking, which gets him into trouble with the media, but at least you know he speaks what's on his mind.

Jesus encouraged my curiosity. When he left earth, he was able to moderate my curiosity through the Holy Spirit. He was able to help me put some thought into the consequences of some of the things I said. I learned over time to temper and moderate what I had to say in the best interests of the people listening.

In the same way, Matthew has learned not to mention the name of the politician in his example that we just shared not to put off people who vote a different way and don't vote for that particular person. We all have a choice in in the things that we say and the way that we say things. Some people say they can't help saying certain things. The fact of the matter is that they're not thinking about the consequences of what they have to say. You can have some sort of control over what you say.

Jesus tried to change me a little bit when we were walking with him, and it had some effect, but I mostly changed through the influence of the Holy Spirit when Jesus left the earth. The Holy Spirit gave me supernatural wisdom and direction. We all know that Solomon was imbued with wisdom from the Holy Spirit and become really wise, so much so that the Queen of Sheba came and visited him, gave him gifts, and wanted to learn from him. He had such a great reputation. It's true that the Holy Spirit can impart wisdom to us and use us.

My curiosity was always active, no matter who I was with and who I was listening to. I was always curious. I moderated some of the things I said and some of the ways that I said things in the future as I progressed from being a follower to actually becoming a leader in Israel, a leader of the church in Jerusalem.

I grew up in some respects. I became more mature. With the help of the Holy Spirit, I became a whole lot more beneficial to the church than this immature person asking what was perceived to be silly questions and saying some things that weren't beneficial to people. I hope that answered your question sufficiently, Rebecca.

Question 4. You walked on water and started sinking. What was that like?

First of all, let me share some background with you to set up the story. Jesus had been on a mountain praying, and we, the disciples, were rowing back in the boat to get back to him to pick him up. We came across a buffeting wind, a storm, that was stopping us from getting the boat to the shore. We were delayed but were trying hard. We saw what we assumed was a ghost in the water.

For those who don't believe in ghosts and think that ghosts are demons, you have to question why the writers of the gospels said that it was a ghost and not a demon. We knew what a demon was. Ghosts have always existed for people who are curious about that.

I recognized Jesus, and he told me to come on the water. He spoke his word. There are many words in the Bible. There are many promises in the Bible that if you have faith, you can supernaturally walk on those promises and find steady ground. You can be in an impossible situation and quote a scripture that applies to that situation and supernaturally walk on the scripture rather than sink in your situation.

I stepped out of the boat. I'd gone about six feet. The storm, the waves, looked really threatening, and I started to fear. I would like to say something about this point. Today I have a chance to address this and speak to all those people who've listened to sermons about this. I'd like to point out that I was the only disciple that wanted to walk on the water, and I was the only disciple that left the boat. The rest were fearfully sitting in the boat.

I walked on water for a little while, and then I sank. Jesus was about twenty feet away when I sank. When I started to sink, I didn't look back to the boat, which would be natural for a fisherman. In most cases, the others might throw a line out of the boat to him and pull him back to the boat. I looked to Jesus, and he zipped across the water and picked me up and had something to say to me. Then he pulled me out of the water, and hand in hand, we walked back to the boat on the water.

Actually I walked on the water twice, once until I sank and once hand in hand with Jesus, the Word of God. I walked out on Jesus's Word, "Come here." But then I doubted the word that allowed me to walk on the water just like the promises of God can help you walk on water. (See Matthew 14:22-33.)

If you claim the promises of God over your life, you can do supernatural things. But if you let the circumstances of your life dictate your beliefs, you become fearful in these situations, and you take your eyes off the promises of God. Then you'll sink, and you'll be overcome by life and your circumstances. But if you place your faith in the Word of God like I placed my faith in the word from Jesus when he said, "Come," then you'll be safe and secure through your travels and in your experiences in life.

I get upset and disturbed by some pastors and people preaching. They attack me. Number one, they don't make it very clear that I was the only disciple that walked on the water that day.

They don't make it clear that I had a lot of faith even asking Jesus if I could come. They don't make a case that Jesus and I walked back to the boat on the water. They don't make a case that I could've turned around and been put back in the boat by the disciples, but instead I placed my faith in Jesus to rescue me.

They don't understand that this was a real lesson for me and one that I cherished. I still fondly remember this special moment. The people and the preachers of the world seem to see this in a negative light. I witnessed so many people preaching on this subject, and so it was great to give my perspective.

The apostle John was interviewed by Matthew. He expressed that, one day, Jesus took out all the disciples, and all the disciples had a secret wish that they could learn how to walk on water like me, and Jesus took them all out into the boat and had them all walk on water. All the apostles did this. All the disciples remember walking on water. Even Judas walked on water. I suppose when I think of my life and what people say about me, I suppose they say harsher things about Judas.

I want you to stress that, despite circumstances being rough, despite life being full of challenges for you, that the Word of God is safe and secure ground. The promises of God can be fulfilled, can work, and can operate in your life, no matter what's coming against you or what position or place you find yourself in your daily life. The Word of God can be trusted. It can be useful. It can be faithful to you, and it can save you.

It can help you walk on water in life and in your circumstances. You can trust the Word of God to hold you secure in every way. You can trust Jesus will be there for you, and he will come to you when you call him, and he will act on your behalf when you're in trouble. It's the same Jesus. Jesus is the answer. The Word of God is true. I hope that the answer to this question has helped you learn a little bit about me too.

Question 5. How did you feel when Jesus rebuked you?

You might remember that Jesus shared that he was going to die and be crucified, and I said to him that I wouldn't allow that to happen. Jesus said to me, "Get behind me, Satan," and he rebuked me. (See Matthew 16:33.)

Some people who read the scriptures only have a limited account of what Jesus said and did. They actually think that's the only rebuke that Jesus used. Scripture says in John 21:25, "And there are also many other things that Jesus did, which if they were written one by one, I suppose that even the world itself could not contain the books that would be written. Amen."

Jesus rebuked us often, which was just his manner. He was a loving Savior full of grace, and he was full of encouragement and love, but he also called us on our mistakes. When Satan manifested or spoke through us or when our flesh spoke, he didn't just say that was okay. He identified it and called us out.

I heard Jesus rebuke other disciples and even me before that rebuke happened. I just took it on the chin like a boxer takes a punch in the chin. It affects him, and it certainly affected me to be told that I was doing Satan's work.

You remember in the Bible in the gospel account just before that happened, I identified Jesus as the Son of God and the Messiah. He said that, "The Father had revealed that to me and that didn't come from men." (See Matthew 16:17.) I have a lot of wisdom from the time Jesus prayed for the Holy Spirit to have a part in our lives. I was flowing with a lot of the wisdom of God.

A real battle was going on between the wisdom of God in my life, my own fleshly ideas, and Satan's influence in my life. The rebuke was not so much hurtful, but it was a wake-up call. It really was like **bold** letters and an underline in a text or a book that you're reading. If a word has bold letters and is **underlined** in the text of a book that you're reading, you really pay attention to it.

When Jesus said, "Satan, get behind me," this really highlighted what was said. I was able to rethink what he said and do some thinking about how Jesus was going to be crucified. It was like bold letters and an underline for the other disciples to actually hear him say that to me.

I was upset. Anyone is upset when the enemy speaks through them. Matthew can relate to this. At one point, he thought that Jesus had spoken to him but found out later through circumstances that it wasn't Jesus who spoke to him but the enemy. It's upsetting to be influenced and used by the enemy. But when you have Jesus in your life, when you have his help, when you have a relationship with him, and you're used to being moved and directed by the Holy Spirit, then these little hiccups along the way just prove that you're special to God and that you simply have a very real enemy.

Some people might look at that rebuke and think that it really devastated me. Those people don't really know how Jesus behaved. Scriptures tell us in the gospels that Jesus asked us disciples, "You of little faith! How long do I have to bear with you?" (See Matthew 17:17.) Jesus said that quite a number of times.

He didn't hold back. He didn't hold back his love and affection, and he didn't hold back his rebukes. He was very thorough in what he had to say.

If we said something that came from the enemy, if the source of what we said or if the source of our action came from the enemy, Jesus was very clear and quick to identify the source of our actions or the source of what we had to say. He made it so that we made no mistake about the source of what we'd said.

Scripture just so happens to record that I'm rebuked, but it doesn't record the rebukes that others received from Jesus and that he did it often. The reason the rebuke is there is to underline the fact that one of the purposes of Jesus was to die and that Jesus had full knowledge that he would die and take away the sins of the world. This reinforces to readers that Jesus understood that he would die for their sins.

I hope you understand that I wasn't totally cut to the heart, and I didn't want to give up my faith because of that rebuke, but that was certainly a good question.

Matthew's Questions

Question 6. What do you like about heaven?

It's another place, especially when you lived on earth like I did before there were even modern-day toilets. Remember, I lived before computers, printers, any type of sanitation, dishwashers, modern kitchens, cars, and trains. I lived when you have to walk from place to place. Most often, only the wealthy had horses or other transportation.

Life when I lived was pretty rough and hard. When you walked from town to town or city to city and it rained, you got soaked, and if you didn't have a sturdy bag with you, your clothes inside the bag were soaked too. It could be chilly having cold clothes and walking in the rain.

Heaven is just another place. You don't have to go to the bathroom in heaven, but there's food there. I really enjoy my food. I enjoy conversation around eating, eating in general, and conversation in general. I really love talking to people from all different backgrounds. I don't know if you've picked up on it so far in this interview, but I really enjoy hearing myself talk. I really am a people person.

In heaven, there's such a great opportunity to develop very close and intimate friendships with your contemporaries. I don't mix with all the disciples in heaven. The twelve apostles walked around together on earth. Though some of you might think that we're all close friends, we all have certain people that we fellowship with and have come to know really well in the two thousand years since we've been there.

So many people from earth that have died have come into the community and the gathering of people that I know and become friends of mine. I'm a friendly chap, to use an Australian word. I really enjoy people and come alive around them.

I'm a good teacher and like to facilitate small groups of people where people learn, sit around, ask questions and take a course. The best way to say it is that I lead courses like a lecturer in university. But instead of a lecturer at the front with all the people sitting in chairs, listening to him speak, groups of twenty to thirty people sit in round circles in the chairs. I'm just one of the contributors. The people discuss certain information and concepts, and everyone asks their questions, and the group as a whole discusses each subject and each part of the topic. I enjoy doing that.

You remember that I had a lot of questions on earth that I asked Jesus. Matthew knows this, but you might not know it. On earth, with Jesus, I was the first person to ask questions when Jesus let us ask questions. I was the first person to try and answer questions. Jesus had to take me aside and tell me not to try and answer the questions first so that the other disciples had a chance to answer the questions.

I started to hold back. That's why, when he asked who he was, I answered the third time because I'd wait to allow other disciples to try and answer the questions. (See Mark 8:27.) Otherwise, I would've said right away, "He was the Messiah and the Son of God."

I enjoy the community of heaven. I enjoy these small group discussions that we have. It's like an intense training going into those group discussions with me, discussing the kingdom. Many people come fresh from earth into one of my small groups, and we discuss certain topics, and people grow a lot.

They all go out to lunch or dinner with their small group. We discuss topics over food, and we grow small little communities in heaven. Then we go to the lecture hall and discuss and learn. That is an interesting aspect of heaven. I really love doing that. I love to teach.

Any good teacher will learn from his students, and many people come into those discussions and actually teach me things. I learned and gleaned from people that have a different take on information. Some people coming from earth really have some novel ideas that might be hard to believe. We haven't thought about them before. You might find these ideas hard to believe.

Earth and heaven are always progressing, and it's so enjoyable to be a part of the small groups in heaven and the way they operate.

Matthew's never heard about this in all the interviews he's done when he's asked what people like about heaven. I really enjoy my job. I really enjoy facilitating those small groups

I enjoy people in heaven like I've told you. I'm really a people person; I really enjoy going out for dinner with people and just how you chew over a bone, and you get every morsel of flesh off the bone. I enjoy having conversations with people like you're chewing on the bone. I like to explore a subject from every dimension. It's interesting to sit down and have dinner and share a meal with someone who knows a lot about a subject and really pick their brain like a bone, to really ask questions and investigate and question them about what they know on the subject.

Kat Kerr has visited heaven thousands of times. She has a lot of knowledge of heaven. Some people in heaven don't possess the knowledge that she has about heaven, and I'd love to sit down with her and pick apart her knowledge of heaven, the knowledge that she's learned speaking with God and Jesus and discuss heavenly concepts with her and have a great time talking back and forth.

As far as Matthew knows, Kat Kerr doesn't have conversations with saints when she goes to heaven, and that is just the way she learns. She simply witnesses what's happening and overhears conversations. I haven't had a conversation with her yet. I look forward to having conversations with her when she passes on or when Jesus returns.

I'm interested in so many people on earth. I would enjoy meeting so many different people, those who have had a real fascination with Jesus and who've developed a really close walk with him. I enjoy meeting people who really love me. I love meeting people who list me as one of their favorite disciples and apostles.

Matthew had a real fascination with me and really loves me. For many years, he felt for me when people preached against me and made harsh statements about my life and what I went through. He has always loved me, so it's a real honor to be in his house and to speak to him.

I love meeting new people. I'm no one special. You don't have to put on airs and graces to meet me. You don't have to bow at my feet and prostrate yourself when you meet me. I'm just a common person. I know a lot about scripture, the Lord, and about heaven. Sometimes I sit on councils in heaven that decide the fate of heaven and earth. I like to be listened to. I like people to consider my opinions, my thoughts, and my contributions.

This is why I really like the small groups that we have because my opinion and my thoughts are considered wisdom by the people that are being taught. They don't have to necessarily agree with everything I have to say, but in heaven, you have to consider that everything that is said is directed by the Holy Spirit. Not many people in heaven are wrong when it comes down to it.

Heaven is a really encouraging place. People are encouraged to be themselves and to shine like the stars. They're led to express themselves and be directed by God to be everything that they were born to be.

Many people don't live the life on earth that they were meant to live, and when they get to heaven, they find out their purpose and their job in heaven. They start to really shine in the dimension that they were meant to shine in on earth. But on earth, they never had the opportunity, never had the knowledge that they were gifted in a certain way. They never shone on earth, but in heaven, everyone is told why they were born. Everyone is given a job to do with excellence, one that they enjoy, and they live this fantastic life, this purpose-driven life in heaven where they enjoy every single day of their existence.

You don't start a day in heaven with regrets, with thinking your job and life are boring or mundane. No feelings like that exist in heaven. Every day is exciting. Everything you do is refreshing. Nothing in heaven is mundane; nothing is without purpose, enjoyment, and love.

Love is dominant in heaven. People are so full of love and so full of enjoyment in what they do and how they express themselves. I hope you've learned some things about heaven, not only what I do with my time in heaven but some other things about heaven as well.

Question 7. What is Jesus like in heaven?

Jesus is the darling of heaven. Heaven revolves around him. Everyone in heaven exists for Jesus's good pleasure, knows him, and meets with him.

Jesus is a different person to everyone in heaven. He remains the same, but people have different experiences of Jesus, depending on their background, what they've been through, and what they've experienced.

If you are a disciple, you knew Jesus on earth and walked with him here. You then lived a life led by the Holy Spirit after he left earth, and you developed a tremendously intimate relationship with Jesus. Your experience with Jesus might be different from someone who just attended church and read their Bible but didn't really know Jesus that well and made it to heaven.

Everyone in heaven gets to experience Jesus at least once a week in earth time, and heaven time is different. But in earth time, they meet Jesus about once a week. He disciples and teaches them. They go to classes during the week, and they learn different things, but everyone in heaven gets to experience Jesus and gets to know him. Everyone in heaven meets Jesus as often as they desire.

It's hard to explain how that works with so many people in heaven, but Jesus is very real to people in heaven. You never tire of meeting him.

Jesus's smile never ends. He smiles a lot. He's full of joy, happiness, contentment, and love. Meeting Jesus and encountering him is so amazing.

He never tires of people. He's never tired, worn down, or burned out. He never acts as if he hasn't had enough sleep, becoming a little snappy or a bit impatient with people.

There's no downside to Jesus. He always has time to see you. You'll never catch him on a bad day.

He's not rebuking people anymore. Everyone in heaven is pretty much led and directed by the Holy Spirit. All their actions tend to align with the Holy Spirit's direction. Jesus isn't rebuking people anymore, telling them, "Get behind me, Satan," like we discussed.

He's always edifying, encouraging, and building people up.

Jesus sees the best in you. He sees your potential and sees where you're headed. He sees the direction that you're going.

He knows where you've come from. He knows everything about your life. He knows all about your life on earth, what you endured, what you suffered, and what you overcame. He knows your life in heaven, what you've learned, and how you've grown.

He speaks to you in that context. He has your previous life and who you are in context. He speaks in that context to you about your week since you last saw him. He speaks encouraging words, words of direction, and instruction toward your future week, your future with him, and your future in heaven.

He is really enjoyable to listen to. Other saints have mentioned it, but you might not have read those books. But when Jesus speaks to you, you hold his undivided attention. Other people could walk past or look at him. They might come up to try to talk to him, and he focuses wholly on you.

When you have his attention, he doesn't shift and talk to other people. He doesn't become distracted by people walking past him. All his attention is on you. It's like you're the center of his universe at that moment. When he breaks off and starts talking to someone else, they become the center of his universe, and you can't distract him when he's with them.

It's different when he's speaking to a crowd because he's directing his speech to the whole crowd, and from time to time, he'll focus on one person in the crowd. But when he's speaking to an individual, that individual is like the center of his universe, and they know it. You know it when he speaks to you. You're really assured, and you can be very confident that when Jesus speaks to you, you're the center of his attention, and he's really enjoying you, loving on you, and showing the wonders of who he is and what he's all about.

Question 8. What must a person do to go to heaven?

It's essential for you to know who Jesus is, to confess that Jesus Christ is the Son of God, and to believe that Jesus Christ died for your sins and rose again, coming back from death. You must believe these things. Then you need to ask Jesus to come and be a part of your life and direct your life.

There's also something to be said about continuing in the faith. Many people start a Christian life and difficulties come up. They become distracted; they turn away from Jesus or don't pay attention to him or to their faith. Some people go to different churches, and people in the church are rude to them. The church might have an oppressive culture that preaches some pretty alarming things, and the person is turned off by church and doesn't attend any more.

You don't specifically have to go to church to be a Christian and to go to heaven. But it's very helpful for you to mix with Christians and have a relationship with others where you can grow. Like I said, in heaven, I run small groups, and we get together in a circle and discuss the Christian faith and things about heaven.

It's very helpful for people to attend those lectures, for them to attend those meetings. Similarly, it is helpful for you to mix with Christians so that you can ask questions, grow, and participate fully in what you believe.

It's helpful for you to read books and to read the Bible. When you're new to the Bible, it will help if you buy a [commentary Bible with notes from Joyce Meyer](#) or someone contemporary that can explain the verses to you. It's helpful for you to learn to hear God speak, and Matthew has a book on how to hear God speak called [*How to Hear God's Voice: Keys to Conversational Two-Way Prayer*](#). It's helpful for you to develop an ability to be able to speak to God and to Jesus and to be able to journal back and forth and record a journal with your conversations with God.

Reading the Bible is wonderful, but it comes with practice and discipline. It takes a while to develop the capacity to be able to be led by the Holy Spirit in reading the Bible. Many people can read God's Word but find it very dry and hard to read. It takes growth and a maturity in the faith to develop to such a stage where the Bible comes alive, and it's active and really refreshing to read.

It helps for you to develop intimacy with Jesus. Matthew has a book called [*7 Keys to Intimacy with Jesus*](#). He has another book called [*Finding Intimacy with Jesus Made Simple*](#). Both of those books would encourage you. [*Jesus Speaking Today*](#) would also help you as well as the *Conversations with God* series ([*Book 1*](#), [*Book 2*](#), and [*Book 3*](#)). These will also encourage you to grow in intimacy with Jesus.

Intimacy with Jesus is powerful and should be encouraged. If you have an intimate relationship with him, you'll enjoy praise and worship and sermons at church. The closer you are to Jesus, the more intimate you are with him, the more you are enjoying worship at church, the more you'll enjoy reading the Bible, the more you'll enjoy church. Your whole Christian experience will be enhanced the closer you are to Jesus.

It's helpful for you to hear some teaching on giving and be able to find a space in your budget to give to God. Many people have an issue with giving, and I encourage you to read books about people who give and who teach on giving. It's really rewarding to live a life where you're free with your money, especially toward God. Andrew Wommack has an excellent book on giving called *Financial Stewardship*.

You need to believe in Jesus and follow him to go to heaven, but reading your Bible, talking to God back and forth, journaling your prayers back and forth to God, giving, being part of small groups, and being part of a church fellowship are all helpful. I'll pray that you can develop and grow in all those aspects of the Christian faith in your life.

JEFF'S QUESTIONS

Question 9. What was your daily walk with Jesus like? How could you put this into words for us who are seeking God's kingdom, God, Jesus, and the Holy Spirit?

A. What was your walk with Jesus like on earth?

Jesus was the most fascinating person that you could ever meet. He was a wonderful man. He was very much otherworldly.

Some people comment to a person, "Get your head out of the clouds." They're actually telling the person to stop following their imagination, stop living in another world, stop daydreaming. Jesus was very much in another world. He used to say that he was bringing the kingdom near, but it was very obvious that he came from another kingdom.

Jesus was from another world. It was very obvious as you were speaking to him that he was hearing from God. It was very clear that God in heaven was his Father, and Jesus took directions from him.

Everything Jesus did was perfect. Even his rebuke was perfect. It was well ordered; it was needed, and it was necessary. You'll notice what he said in the Bible when the woman came to him to heal her child. He said he doesn't give the children's bread to the dogs. (See Mark 7:28.) The woman could've been offended that Jesus was saying that people of another race are dogs, but everything was true and correct. She knew that's what Israelites called her race. Yet she pressed on with Jesus, and she received a miracle.

Jesus was very clear. He did everything right. To people who were religious, Jesus was outspoken, and he was contrary to what they taught.

Jesus walked with a lot of authority. He was hard to disagree with. You'd have to have real courage, tenacity, and inner strength to disagree with him. The authorities and the teachers of the law took it upon themselves to disagree with him. Jesus sometimes rebuked them and sometimes asked them questions to stump them and make them feel and look foolish.

You have to understand that the Jewish custom of that day in teaching was to ask questions and to be asked questions. It was more of a discussion like I have in heaven with my students. It was not so much one person preaching with everyone listening but an active discussion.

My life was all about Jesus, and it was just so beneficial for me. I wished I had Jesus all to myself on earth. Jesus was often busy with people, doing things, and talking to different people. I sometimes wished in my flesh that I had more of Jesus to myself. I wished that I could ask him more questions. I wished he could answer all my questions.

He didn't always answer all my questions. I wanted to ask a question, and he wouldn't call on me to ask my question. Some of my questions went unanswered.

Of course, when he left, I was able to ask the Holy Spirit questions that came to mind. My mind was always active and running. Everything Jesus did caused another question to pop up in me, "Why did he do that? Why did he say that? What does he mean by that?"

I don't know. Matthew is a lot like me with a lot of questions. He's learned to ask Jesus questions, listen to the Holy Spirit, do his own research, and read books, and slowly his questions are being answered. I had a lot of questions for Jesus on earth.

I really enjoyed Jesus. His words were living water. It was like it says in the passage in John 7:38 that out of his belly will flow springs of living water. This referred to the Holy Spirit, who just flowed out of him in a beautiful stream of inspiration and revelation.

You couldn't capture everything Jesus said. Sometimes he spoke for five or six hours or longer. We didn't have iPhones to record it. We didn't have video to capture what Jesus said.

What you didn't record, you lost. It was just like it was gone; it was an overflow of information. It's taken me two thousand years in heaven to catch up, to have all of my questions answered, and still, questions remain.

Jesus is continually a mystery to me in heaven, and he's continually full of revelation. There's no end to the knowledge that Jesus possesses in heaven. He's just the central focal point of heaven.

Jesus was very wise, practical, and full of information. He taught me to heal and how to deal with demons. He taught me to teach people a message and taught me how to structure a message to have a few points and build on each point. He told me, rather showed me, how to give a message for thirty minutes or for three hours, and it'd be the same message but just more complex and profound.

He taught me a lot of things. He took me aside and personally coached me and showed me what I needed to know for my future.

He understood my future and what I'd need. He understood the questions that really needed answering right now, and he made sure to answer those questions.

He was a very personable God and friend. I count it a real honor to call him friend. He really was the best person I've ever met in my life and still remains my favorite person in the world.

B. How was your walk with Jesus after he left?

It came to a day when Jesus was crucified, which was a hard day. I'm going to talk about my denial of him in a later question, but there was a day when Jesus rose again, came back, talked to us, and filled us up with some information, and then ascended and went back to heaven. There was a void for forty days, and then the Holy Spirit came at Pentecost.

I was full of questions. You may have noticed that I had a lot of questions and was encouraged to be a teacher who gave a lot of information when he preached. I was a detail-oriented person, and I liked to know the nitty-gritty and everything there is to know about a subject.

I really drew on the Holy Spirit. Some people have the Holy Spirit in their lives and don't really use him. They're not really directed by the Holy Spirit. Jesus said that the Holy Spirit would be our helper. He said that the Holy Spirit will lead us into all truth and all information. (See John 16:13.) He told us that he needed to leave so that the Holy Spirit could come.

I remembered his words as recorded in John 14. This happened after the Last Supper but before he was taken and betrayed. He told us all this information about the Holy Spirit.

I had a dire need for the Holy Spirit. Some people might have nice expensive plates in their house but rarely take out the plates and use them. Some people might not have normal dishes, so they use the expensive plates all the time because that's all they have. I was desperate. I didn't have the normal plates but was always using expensive plates.

My life was totally wrecked without Jesus. Not wrecked because Jesus understood that he had to leave and leave us the Holy Spirit, but I really needed the Holy Spirit and his influence in my life.

Jesus was a great message to preach. His understanding of the kingdom was the best understanding possible. His lifestyle, his way of life, the way that he taught us to live was so far-reaching and so far advanced when compared with the modern Judaism that we lived under. It was so radical, so new, and so refreshing to live that way.

You have a better understanding of what Jesus meant if you read Jesus's commands that you can find in the link here. If you live according to these commands and what Jesus taught, your life will be better. If you read Jesus's parables found in Matthew's book, *The Parables of Jesus Made Simple: Updated and Expanded Edition*, then you will better appreciate what Jesus taught and what he was all about.

When you understand what Jesus taught, what he preached, and the lifestyle of Christianity, you will find that it's extraordinary, that it's radically different from the way that we've lived before. I wanted to preach this message. The Holy Spirit empowered me and gave me inspiration to speak.

I learned to be directed by the Holy Spirit. I learned to have my words filled in by the Holy Spirit just as Matthew is answering these questions, and my words are directed by the Holy Spirit as coming through Matthew. I'm speaking only as I am directed by the Holy Spirit.

It's a real lesson for Matthew to be able to sit back and hear me speak. He's chosen to do this, but it's done by faith. The same is true when the Holy Spirit is guiding what you have to say. You don't have notes. You don't come to a pulpit with notes, but you come with scripture verses, and the Holy Spirit just takes control of your mouth, and you start to speak.

I was very dependent on the Holy Spirit. I chose to use the Holy Spirit as my holy trainer, as my teacher and counselor. I didn't have anything else. I had no Plan B or any other option.

I couldn't go back to the life that I lived. I couldn't live with myself as a fisherman. I had to go forward and do what Jesus was leading me to do.

I had to share the beautiful message of Jesus with the other Jews and people in society. I had to share the message of Jesus with the Gentiles. I had to share the tremendous life of Jesus and the way that he taught us to live, the better way of living, the more fulfilling way of living with the people that didn't have any idea of the light, that didn't have any idea of the way, that had no understanding of the truth.

Jesus was the way, the truth, and the life. (See John 14:6.) He was the way to live your life. He showed us truth. He showed us the only sustaining way to live your life. He showed us the way that we're meant to live.

I took hold of that life. I took those lessons that we learned from Jesus, and I took them to the people. I heavily depended on the Holy Spirit to give me the direction and the words to say.

Question 10. Can you describe the love of God and Jesus for his children?

The best way to explain it is as if you are a parent, if you have children. The love that you have for a child is a very special sort of love. The child can break your heart. The child can fail in exams. The child can fail to apply themselves at school. The child can get into drugs or sexual misconduct.

No matter what the child does, you love the child. You have a very great love for your child.

If you don't have children, you might compare it to loving an animal that you own: a dog, cat, or canary. The love of God is similar to that but richer, much richer. You might love a friend that you've grown up with or a friend you've met at school or at work who you've talked with lots in deep and meaningful conversations. God loves you like you love your friend but even more. You might love a boyfriend or a girlfriend, and you've shared sweet times together, holding hands, kissing each other, with many great conversations over a meal. The love of God is stronger than that.

Love is an amazing thing, and yet there's no love like the love that God has for his people. You can't compare the love that you have for a favorite pet. You can't compare the love you have for a spouse. You can't compare the love you even have for a child to the love that God has for us.

I've spoken to God. I've sat on Jesus's throne and sat on God's lap. The universe just stops when he talks to you. Just like Jesus, when you're talking to God, nothing else exists. You could have a whole throne room of people worshipping God. When you're speaking to him face to face, nothing else matters.

He loves you, dear reader, so completely. He just loves you. It's really hard to describe his love outside of experience. Someone can talk about surfing, what a joy it is to surf, and how much fun it is to surf. They can show you pictures of surfing and show you a movie of surfers. You can have a dramatic movie of surfers going to a certain spot and paddling out to surf. But you don't really understand surfing until you put the effort into learning how to surf. You start to surf, and you start to ride the waves and experience a good wave for yourself. You don't fully understand surfing until you've tried it. Matthew's been a surfer, so he knows what it's like.

The same is true with God's love. As a Christian, you experience a dimension of it. As you grow in intimacy as a Christian, you experience more of it. Matthew has three books, a series on *Conversations with God*: [Book 1](), [Book 2](), and [Book 3](). In those three books, you can read how Matthew speaks to God and how God is his friend. He has a personal experience of how God loves him and how God talks with him friend to friend.

You really need to experience God and his love just like you really need to experience surfing to understand surfing.

The same can be said about eating shellfish. You can explain that it tastes really fishy. The taste is quite different. But you won't understand what it really tastes like until you actually experience eating it. You might understand that it's too rich for you to eat often. You might experience shellfish and not ever want to eat it again. God's love needs to be experienced and explored.

God's love is like honey. Honey never grows old. It never has to be thrown out because it's too old. It's sweet, dependable, and sustainable. You will never have to throw him out.

Jesus's love is the same. I went into this in detail about how Jesus treats you in heaven. Jesus loved us so much that he came to earth to die. He came to earth not only to die and to make a way for a relationship with God, but he came to earth to model what it's like to be a Christian, what it's like to be a follower of God.

Jesus loves you so much. He allows Matthew to spend thousands of dollars so that you hear the message of this book. He loves you so much that he'll invest in you. It might cost you ninety-nine cents to buy this book, but Jesus loves you with thousands of dollars spent to actually make this book happen.

The love of the Trinity is indescribable. It needs to be experienced. Have you experienced God's love? Do you know that he loves you? You might know that he loves you. Have you experienced his love?

I encourage you all to start to journal and to record your prayers, writing what God has to say to you.

Question 11. When you experienced your heart break after denying Jesus three times, what change in insight did you have? How did your feelings change? What battles did you face? Did you know God would forgive you?

I have experienced various events on earth a number of times. I've seen thousands of people preach about when I denied Jesus. The Holy Spirit gave Matthew insight years ago and said that the reason I denied Jesus three times was because I was the only disciple that was following and watching what happened to him. All the other disciples, including John, had run away.

Let me walk you through this situation. Imagine if you were there, and you didn't run away, but you followed Jesus and watched him go from place to place as he was questioned. What would you say if someone asked, "Were you with Jesus?" knowing that he'd been arrested and a whole lot of soldiers had captured him? What would you say? Would you honestly say, "Yes, I'm one of Jesus's closest disciples?" Would you risk your life, or would you lie like I did?

I'm not sure that many people would have told the truth if they were in the same circumstances as I was. I want you to consider something as a reader. First of all, would you have followed after Jesus to where he was being questioned? Or would you have fled with the rest of the disciples in fear?

Because understandably, they did flee in fear. They didn't have to stand up to people's questions about who they were because they weren't there when Jesus was being questioned.

Secondly, if you didn't flee, if you did what I did, and if you were trying to keep your promise that you'd never leave him, would you answer that question, saying, "Yes, I am one of his closest disciples," or would you lie like I did? I just want to put that into this book for you to ponder.

It broke my heart to deny Jesus. I didn't fully understand what Jesus said when he said, "Before the cock crows, you'll deny me three times." You don't understand some things right away. But later, the Holy Spirit opens your understanding. I only understood Jesus's words after I had just finished denying him for the third time, and the cock crowed, and I remembered what Jesus said.

It broke my heart. I didn't feel that God wouldn't forgive me. I already knew what his forgiveness was like. You have to understand Jesus. If you've looked into Jesus's eyes, if you've had his arm around you, if you had heard some of the things he'd said to me, you'd understand that you could pretty much do anything and be forgiven by Jesus.

But I was heartbroken with myself. I had denied him. I had said that I didn't know Jesus, and that was real. That was something I couldn't take back. But I didn't feel in any way that I'd lost my relationship with Jesus. I didn't feel like Jesus wouldn't forgive me for that.

It was a real wake-up call when the cock crowed, and I remembered what Jesus had said. Even Jesus had the foreknowledge that I would deny him. It gave me comfort in a way to know that Jesus already knew I would deny him.

Jesus had told me that Satan had asked to sift me and that he'd given Satan permission and that I'd overcome. I understood this denial of Jesus was part of his sifting. I understood that I would overcome.

How would you feel if you denied Jesus? Jesus said very clearly in the parable of the sheep and the goats in Matthew 25:31-46, "What you did to the least of my brethren, you did unto me." Nearly everyone reading this book has had a homeless person ask them for spare change, and they have said "no" and denied a homeless person.

Nearly everyone who's reading this book has denied someone that Jesus sent to them for help. Matthew knows that he has. Nearly all of us, if we're honest with ourselves, have denied Jesus in some way through not giving charity to someone else.

I suppose it's easy to look at my denial of Jesus and say, "I would never do that." But if Jesus says what you do to the least of my brethren, you do unto me, and you look at how many times you've denied a poor person or a homeless person change, you may realize that you've denied Jesus a whole lot more than I did. You may say to yourself, "Well, that wasn't Jesus. That was just a homeless person." I suppose that's up to your own conscience to decide.

I want to leave you with these questions. If you were the disciples, would you have fled with the other disciples in fear, including John? Or would have you done what I did and followed Jesus and then, when people asked you, confessed and said, "Yes, I'm one of Jesus's closest disciples?"

Because if you can answer yes, you wouldn't have done what I did and you wouldn't have denied Jesus, well, in that instance, you're a better person than I am. I have no shame about denying Jesus. Satan did this to sift me, and it was true that it happened. I'm not justifying my actions, but I learned so much from it.

I am very proud of who I am, and I am not ashamed of what I did. I'm fully redeemed and fully forgiven by Jesus. Whether you know it or not, our relationship became stronger because of what I did.

Question 12. How will I know when I talk to Jesus versus talking to the Father and not show any disrespect to either?

This is an interesting question. First of all, the question is how do you know when you're speaking to Jesus or when you're speaking to the Father? Matthew finds a difference in the resonance of the voices. In Matthew's experience, the Father speaks with more authority than Jesus. That's how he knows the Father is speaking. I have to agree that the Father always spoke to me with more authority.

But if you mistake whose voice it is, neither Jesus nor the Father are offended. Jesus and the Father are one. If you've spoken to Jesus, you've spoken to the Father.

At one time, Matthew spoke to the Father for the first time. The Father reminded him that, whenever he was speaking to Jesus, he was speaking to him, and he'd been speaking to him for years. That little revelation of truth resounded with Matthew and really impacted him. Matthew had assumed that he'd been speaking to Jesus for thirty years, and God wasn't really listening. The fact was that, because Jesus and the Father are one, he was really speaking to the Father all the time that he was speaking to Jesus.

Rest assured, Jeff, that when you speak to Jesus, you are speaking to the Father. When you are speaking to the Father, Jesus is listening, and you are speaking to Jesus. The Father and Jesus aren't offended in any way if you mistake who's speaking to you.

They might correct you. If you start referring to the Father as Jesus during a conversation, the Father might correct you and say, "This is the Father," and vice versa. If you're speaking to who you assume is the Father, and it's actually Jesus, Jesus might correct you and say, "This is Jesus."

Certainly, feel free to ask them, "Who am I speaking to, Jesus or the Father?" They're quite patient and understanding. They'll tell you who you're speaking to as long as you're speaking to one of them.

I had a really dynamic relationship with Jesus, the Father, and the Holy Spirit when I was on earth. I was able to identify the Holy Spirit's voice. I could hear him speak. I could dictate what the Holy Spirit speaks just like Matthew's dictating what I have to say here.

I was able to speak with the intuition of the Holy Spirit and to speak prophetically as the Holy Spirit spoke. I could talk to Jesus in heaven. I was able to have a conversation with the Father in heaven and speak back and forth with him.

If the Father or Jesus in heaven ever spoke to me and I was wrong, all was forgiven. There was nothing to forgive. In fact, they understand that we have human frailties, human misunderstandings, and the way that we operate as humans. They totally understand, and they teach us how to know them better.

You couldn't show disrespect to Jesus by addressing him as the Father. You can address the Father as Jesus and show no disrespect. When you talk to Jesus and speak to him all the time, you are not showing disrespect to the Father. Jesus and the Father are happy when you're speaking to them. It's not a matter of them being upset when you talk to either of them.

You are obviously showing respect when you speak to the Father. He has more authority and more power than Jesus, but there's no such thing as disrespecting him because you're laboring or spending more time speaking to one or the other.

Some people have had difficult circumstances with their own fathers and find it harder to have a loving and easy relationship with the Heavenly Father. Matthew was that way for many years and still speaks to Jesus a lot more than he speaks to the Father, but he's being healed, and he's growing in that area.

The Father doesn't feel slighted or upset in any way that Matthew speaks to Jesus more than to him. Both God and Jesus are very happy when someone's speaking to them rather than just going on with the affairs of the world, doing things in the world, and operating in the flesh as it were. They're very interested in people interacting with them, dialoguing with them, and talking to them.

Question 13. What is the best advice you can give in order to grow intimate with Jesus, God, and the Holy Spirit?

Well, how do you become intimate with your girlfriend or your wife? I know that sex is one way to be intimate, but I'm not talking about that. How do a boyfriend and a girlfriend grow intimate? Don't they talk to each other?

One of the best ways to become close to another person is by talking and listening to them. Now you might not consider that you can talk and listen to the Holy Spirit, but you really can. Many people live a Christian life, and they don't have conversations with Jesus. They don't have conversations with the Father or with the Holy Spirit.

They live in somewhat of a vacuum. They go to church. They read the Bible, and they pray these one-way prayers.

Matthew calls them one-way prayers because that's what they are. They are one-way conversations. Can you imagine sitting down with your girlfriend or your wife and just speaking at her, not allowing her to answer any of your questions, not allowing her to speak back at all, but just telling her all the things you did wrong that day or that week and then asking her for a whole lot of other things? But whenever she wants to speak, you put up your hand and say, "No, don't speak." What sort of relationship would you have with your loved one if you did that? Yet many Christians do that all the time.

When I was on earth, I had such a dynamic relationship with Jesus. Like I said, I spent so much time asking Jesus questions and wishing that I had more of Jesus to myself. When he left, a void was in my life that was filled by the Holy Spirit. I really relied on the Holy Spirit in a powerful way because of the void left in my life.

I learned to listen to the Holy Spirit. I learned to be directed by the Holy Spirit. I learned through speaking to the Holy Spirit that I was able to connect with Jesus and speak to him.

The relationship I had with Jesus didn't diminish when he left. It actually improved my relationship with the Godhead. I not only spoke to Jesus and to the Father, but I had this improved relationship with the Holy Spirit.

I have to say, before we finish this question, that one way of growing your relationship with the Father, Jesus, and the Holy Spirit is to obey. Jesus says in John 14:21, "He who has My commandments and keeps them, it is he who loves Me. And he who loves Me will be loved by My Father, and I will love him and manifest Myself to him."

Jesus spoke this passage in John between when he ate the last supper and when he was taken in the garden. He says quite clearly here that if you love him, you will obey his commandments. The fact that the Father and Jesus will love you more if you obey them hints that there'll be a greater love from Jesus and the Father if you obey the commandments. It certainly says that you'll be loved by them if you obey.

What if your wife often asked you to do things? What if she wanted you to do things for her? What if you always ignored what she said she wanted you to do, and you never did what she asked? Would your relationship start to break down? Would there be some cracks in your relationship?

Well, Jesus has clearly expressed in the gospels what we need to do. If you check out the [fifty commands of Jesus](), you'll find that Jesus had fifty things that he told his disciples to do. When you start to obey Jesus and what he taught, when you realize that Jesus only taught what the Father was saying, you will realize that you're obeying the Father when you're obeying Jesus. It will improve your relationship with both Jesus and the Father.

What if you learn to hear the Holy Spirit? What if you learn to be directed by the Holy Spirit? Do you think that your relationship with the Holy Spirit will improve if you start to obey his leadings and do what the Holy Spirit is directing you to do?

You can speak to them and get to know them. This certainly works for people. The more that they speak to each other, the more they dialogue back and forth with each other, the closer they become. People also improve in their relationships when they do things for each other that the other person asks of them.

These are two of my best suggestions for you. I encourage each of you to take out a journal and journal with God, Jesus, and the Holy Spirit if you want to grow in your relationship with them. Ask them questions, speak to them, and write down what each of them says to you. I encourage you to learn how to hear from God. You can buy Matthew's book, *How to Hear God's Voice*, if you click on this link.

I encourage you to speak to God, to journal with God. I encourage you to start to listen to the directions that come from God and start to obey them, and you'll grow in your relationship.

Question 14. Where and how do I learn to draw closer to the Trinity in order to hear their voices distinctly and know that I'm doing God's will? I want to be in sync with them like Jesus was with God.

I first heard Jesus's voice. I didn't hear the voice of the Holy Spirit until Jesus prayed for us to be led by the Holy Spirit. But first, I heard Jesus's voice and then came the voice of the Holy

Spirit. After Pentecost, the voice of the Father started to interact with me.

It helps if you know one of them first. If you know the voice of Jesus very clearly, then when the Holy Spirit or the Father speaks, it will have a different sound to it even though the sound is resonating in your own thoughts. The thought will have a different resonance. You can ask the Holy Spirit and the Father to speak to you, or you can address the Holy Spirit and the Father and ask them to confirm that it's really them speaking to you when you're talking. You can start the conversation with addressing the Holy Spirit, the Father, or Jesus and then have them confirm to you that they are speaking back.

Like anything, if you're a chef, you make your pie, and you cut it into slices. If you have a particular size for a slice as a chef, if you ever see one of your assistants or one of your other chefs serve a slice of pie that's little smaller or larger than your perfect slice, you'll notice the difference right away. You might call the pie back and have a perfect slice cut instead.

Like the perfect pie piece, if you don't know the voice of Jesus very well, you might not be able to distinguish the voice of the Holy Spirit or of the Father that well. When you are familiar with the one member of the Trinity, you will learn the difference between them all.

If I were you, I'd concentrate on learning one of the voices really well. I'd start with Jesus. The Holy Spirit can lead you through your intuition to start a conversational relationship with Jesus.

I'd start to journal with Jesus. You could start with the Holy Spirit or with the Father also. But it will be good for you start with Jesus and do a hundred pages of speaking back and forth to him.

Then start your second one hundred pages of speaking to the Father and Jesus and learn to distinguish between them both.

No one reads the instructions for golf and goes out and plays a perfect round of golf. In fact, people can read all the books that they like about golf and never improve in their game. You can even play golf and not improve because you don't play regularly. Most people don't ever become good golfers until someone instructs and teaches them the proper way to swing and how to hold themselves correctly.

Like everything, even a game like golf, you need experience. You can't just read a book with me, telling you how to speak to the Father, how to speak to Jesus, and how to speak to the Holy Spirit and hear their voices clearly and accurately on the first try. You need practice and experience. Just as any golfer can learn the fundamentals in a book, the experience that he has playing the game actually teaches him.

A golfer can play once a week and stay at the same level that he is. But in golf, unless you play two or three times a week, you're generally not going to improve your game.

The same is true with speaking to the Godhead. If you're only speaking to them once a week, you might not improve your ability. But if you're speaking to them every day and practicing speaking to them, you'll improve.

I can say it a hundred times, which might annoy people. But Matthew has said it a number of times in his other books. The best way to improve your ability to speak to the Godhead is to just speak to them. You can speak to them back and forth in your mind, but when you document what you hear, it's really beneficial, and it acts like a memoir or a record of your history with the Trinity to read over if you use a journal.

You can write a journal or dictate onto Microsoft Word and then send it to a spiritually mature friend and ask, "Do you think that this is really God speaking? Which parts of it do you think are God speaking, and what parts am I just saying myself? Which parts do you think are God, or do you think it's all God speaking?" You can check that out with a trusted person. You can have someone check over what you're hearing so that it's not delusional, and you don't become deceived. Matthew goes into detail about that in his book, *How to Hear God's Voice*.

That's my advice to you. You could never play in a world championship of golf without practicing two to three times a week or without being taught by a professional instructor to eliminate all the bad habits from your game. You could never expect to play in a championship and even win a championship without plenty of experience. The same is true with God and your communication. I hope I've reinforced this to you when it comes to speaking to the Godhead.

You can develop an ability to hear the Holy Spirit and hear Jesus speak so that you can walk like Jesus. It says in 1 John 2:6, "He who says he abides in Him ought himself also to walk just as He walked." John was saying that it's possible to walk like Jesus.

The apostle Paul said in 1 Corinthians 11:1, "Imitate me as I imitate Christ." It's possible to be like Paul and imitate and walk like Christ. It is possible to be like Jesus. It's not strange for you to want to be like Jesus, but everything comes from experience.

Question 15. How do I seek God with all my heart? What does that mean?

You have to get your life to a place where everything you're doing revolves around promoting God and his glory. So you need to shift your priorities so that everything you're doing affects the kingdom. This includes your life when you're at work doing your job. You do the job unto the Lord and for him. Do your job with excellence, and treat people with dignity and honor and how you'd like to be treated.

So if you're doing a job in the marketplace with excellence, the other employees and your boss will notice if you have an attitude of doing it for God. You are then actually doing ministry. If you do it with excellence, people will take notice, and they'll see that you're a diligent worker. If you treat people in your job with love and compassion, forgive people, and don't gossip, then you will make an impact.

If you serve your wife like Jesus served the church when he died and gave his life for her, then your relationship with your wife will improve. If you seek God on what you should do for your wife, how you should treat her, what surprises you should buy for your wife, what little things you can do that will bless her, God will see that your marriage is blessed.

If you seek God in little things, if you seek him in what TV shows to watch, what books to read, what YouTube videos to watch, if you seek him in everything, then you will fulfill seeking God with all your heart.

God is not boring. God doesn't have a problem with you watching certain TV shows or movies that don't even talk about Christ. Some people are really religious and really stuck in their ways, and they won't watch any TV or see movies. God is not like that; God wants you to be able to relate to people in the world.

Matthew is watching a series called *NCIS* at the moment, and it's amazing how many conversations he's been able to have with people simply by discussing that TV show. He's talked to about five different people about that show, and they've all watched it and liked it. Apparently, it was once the highest rated show on American TV, but Matthew is talking to people in Australia.

So it's okay to be doing worldly things like watching TV and still serve God. Matthew will watch *NCIS* and be emotionally affected by scenes in the show, breaking down in tears, and God uses the show to minister to him.

You want to make the focus of your life on God. One thing that you can do is set a target and set some goals of what you want to achieve in your Christian life. Do you recognize someone who is an exemplary model of a Christian? What do they do? What are they involved in? What do they watch? Who did they like? Who are the preachers that they read, that they listen to? Who is someone that you really admire? Do you admire Matthew? Who are the preachers that he listens to? What books does he read? What does he do? If you learn to model your life after what is working and what's successful for other people, then that will change your life.

What does it mean to seek God with all your heart? It is essentially having God as the center of your universe and understanding that he can have as much or little control in your life as you allow him. We as humans all have free will. It's a real change to come to earth and speak to someone here because, in heaven, everything is centered on God or on Jesus, and people don't need to learn how to seek God with all their heart. But on earth, you have free will, and you can choose to order your life in an exemplary way that serves God and that is a demonstration of his kingdom to everyone else.

So find out who you admire as a Christian, write to them, and ask questions like the following: Who are your favorite speakers? Who are your favorite writers? What would you suggest that I do to change my life to be more focused on God? There you go.

Question 16. If I surrender my all to God, does that mean I will lose my wife, family, and job to do his will?

If you understand anything about God, you'll understand that God is really all about family. Abraham was called to leave his family, but he still took Lot with him. The Bible doesn't have many examples where a person loses their wife, family, and job to do God's will.

I had a wife and a mother-in-law. When the children grew up, my wife traveled with me, and we did ministry together. God is not a killjoy. He won't come against your family, your job, or the things that are comfortable in your life so that you can do his will. He might shift your family to another state; he might ask you to do a different job. He might actually call you into the ministry and have you start to live by faith. He might make changes that will affect your family and your wife and what job you do if you honestly want to surrender to his will.

I know many people on earth fear the will of God because they think that God will make drastic changes in their lives. What many people don't understand or don't seem to comprehend is that God's will for their lives is best. God's will for your life, Jeff, is not to disrupt your life and make your life unenjoyable and unsustainable. God's will for your life is to use your talents to the very best of your ability to bring him the maximum glory.

You might be working as an architect, but God's desire might be for you to be an artist. It might be risky for you to leave your high-paying job as an architect to become an unknown artist. It might be risky for a season, but you might find that your art work is outperforming your salary as an architect in five to ten years, and you're bringing glory to the Lord's name.

A shift and a change comes with many things in life if you do them God's way. But God, I'll repeat, is not a killjoy. He doesn't come against people's lives to shift them just for his sake, just to make himself feel better, to make himself happy. I can understand that you have a real fear of losing your family, your wife, and your job to do the will of God, but those fears are more rooted in the flesh and in Satan and not in reality. God has a way that he wants to glorify himself in your life.

Steve Jobs was a successful man who created Apple products and created Pixar Animation, and he did a terrific job on earth. He wasn't a Christian, but he actually brought glory to God with the products that he created. If he was a Christian on earth now, he probably would just change some of the best practices that Apple incorporates and bring changes to his corporation. His products might become more expensive due to using more sustainable and more ethical ways of producing them, but his life might not have to radically change to come into alignment with God.

So you don't have to fear. I'm quite confident I'm sitting here with Jesus. I'm quite confident that you can sing the song "I Surrender All" to Jesus, and he's not going to ruin your life. You have to understand what his will is. Is his will something destructive to you, that is working against you, or is God's will for your life the very best your life can be and the most extraordinary life that you can live?

If God's will is the most extraordinary life that you can live, why not live it? Why not hand over your life to Jesus and say, "Lead me?" And if he wanted you to move to a new state or city, if he's going to have you change jobs, he'd work with you, and you'd have a choice in the matter. He wouldn't just shut down your whole life and destroy it.

I hope this made sense to you. Of course, in heaven, everyone is doing the job that they were created to do. Everyone enjoys what they're doing and really loves their work; they're fully sustained, fully appreciated, and fully engaged in what they're doing in heaven. Jesus would really love for people on earth to be engaged in the jobs that they were created to do. Jesus would really love for people to seek him and shift and move into the correct positions. That really is the answer to your question. Jesus might have something better for you to do, and he might have something else for your wife and your family to do. You might want to seek him out in that area rather than being scared.

I really loved your questions. You had some really thought-provoking questions that stretched Matthew and made him press into the kingdom so that I could answer your questions.

Matthew's Question

Question 17. Do you have any final thoughts?

It was a real honor to come down and speak today. Rebecca and Jeff both had some great questions, personal questions toward the end. It was a real privilege to seek God and spend time answering these personal questions. They're included in the book because I think they are helpful questions for the average Christian to read, and I think that they are helpful for readers to contemplate, especially the message about journaling. This seems to be a recurring message in your books, Matthew, and it's a real privilege to bring that message.

To trust in Jesus means more than knowing things about Jesus, reading books about him, or studying his life. Trusting Jesus is actually doing what Jesus told you to do. So you, the reader, should look up the commands of Jesus, print them out to put on your fridge and start to obey them. You could read the book, *The Parables of Jesus Made Simple: Updated and Expanded Edition*, and you could start to practice the parables and start to live them out. In order to know Jesus, you should really do more than read about him in a book, just like when you learn to play golf, you need to do more than read about it in a book.

It would be really good if you took Jesus's words out and started to put them into practice and started to live a life that made you into a little Christ, that made you into a disciple of Christ. It would be good if you became more than just someone who sits on the pew in church each week but doesn't really do anything with your life when it comes to Christ.

It would be good if you read or listened to books and activated yourself and started to obey what the books had to say. It would be helpful if you made changes in the world, if you were a forerunner, a pioneer, who encouraged and built people up and if you were an example in their community and in their world.

It would be really good if you decided to follow Matthew as an author. It would be really good if you read all of his books. You can even write to him, and he will pay for all your Kindle books if you can't afford them. Matthew is really devoted to the kingdom and to the Lord, and he writes as the Holy Spirit leads him to write. He writes a lot of very helpful and encouraging books on the kingdom for people to read and put into practice.

I encourage you to check out his books. I encourage you to get to know him, and you can even follow him on Amazon so that Amazon sends you an email when a new book of his has been released.

It's been a real privilege and an honor to be here; I've really enjoyed myself. Matthew had the courage to answer these questions that he didn't know the answer to. He really stepped out of the boat on this one.

I'm glad that I got to speak on Jesus's rebuke of me. I'm glad I got to speak about when I sank in the water and about my denial of Jesus three times. I'm glad I had something to say in those three controversial areas and subjects that I don't see treated too well on earth by preachers, and I'm glad I could give my perspective.

I love you. I'll see you all in heaven. Hopefully, one day, you'll join my small group, and we can discuss the Word of God and life in heaven. I hope that I can sit opposite you one day and share the love of Jesus with you and the love that I have for everyone in my heart.

I'D LOVE TO HEAR FROM YOU

One of the ways that you can bless me as a writer is by writing an honest and candid review of my book on Amazon. I always read the reviews of my books, and I would love to hear what you have to say about this one.

Before I buy a book, I read the reviews first. You can make an informed decision about a book when you have read enough honest reviews from readers. One way to help me sell this book and to give me positive feedback is by writing a review for me. It doesn't cost you a thing but helps me and the future readers of this book enormously.

To read my blog, request a life-coaching session, request your own personal prophecy, request a visit to heaven, or to receive a personal message from your angel, you can also visit my website at http://personal-prophecy-today.com All of the funds raised through my ministry website will go toward the books that I write and self-publish.

You can also request a trip to heaven with Robin Gann. You can find her contact information on my website.

To write to me about this book or to share any other thoughts, please feel free to contact me at my personal email address at survivors.sanctuary@gmail.com

You can also friend request me on Facebook at Matthew Robert Payne. Please send me a message if we have no friends in common as a lot of scammers now send me friend requests.

You can also do me a huge favor and share this book on Facebook as a recommended book to read. This will help me and other readers.

How to Sponsor a Book Project

If you have been blessed by this book, perhaps you might consider sponsoring a book for me. It normally costs me between fifteen hundred and two thousand dollars or more to produce each book that I write, depending on the length of the book.

If you seek the Holy Spirit about financing a book for me, I know that the Lord would be eternally grateful to you. Consider how much this book has blessed you and then think of hundreds or even thousands of people who would be blessed by a book of mine. As you are probably aware, the vast majority of my books are ninety-nine cents on Kindle, which proves to you that book writing is indeed a ministry for me and not a money-making venture. I would be very happy if you supported me in this.

If you have any questions for me or if you want to know what projects I am currently working on that your money might finance, you can write to me at survivors.sanctuary@gmail.com and ask me for more information. I would be pleased to give you more details about my projects.

You can sow any amount to my ministry by simply sending me money via the PayPal link at this address: http://personal-prophecy-today.com/support-my-ministry/

You can be sure that your support, no matter the amount, will be used to publish helpful Christian books for people to read.

I am in the process of starting a book-publishing company called Christian Book Publishing USA where I hope to totally finance other people's self-published books with no income for my effort. If you would like to donate to this ministry and the books that I will publish on the behalf of others, please write to me and ask for more information.

Other Books by Matthew Robert Payne

The Prophetic Supernatural Experience

Prophetic Evangelism Made Simple

Your Identity in Christ

His Redeeming Love: A Memoir

Writing and Self-Publishing Christian Nonfiction

Coping with your Pain and Suffering

Living for Eternity

Jesus Speaking Today

Great Cloud of Witnesses Speak

My Radical Encounters with Angels

Finding Intimacy with Jesus Made Simple

My Radical Encounters with Angels: Book Two

A Beginner's Guide to the Prophetic

Michael Jackson Speaks from Heaven

7 Keys to Intimacy with Jesus

Conversations with God: Book 1

Optimistic Visions of Revelation

Conversations with God: Book 2

Finding Your Purpose in Christ

Influencing your World for Christ: Practical Everyday Evangelism

Deep Calls unto Deep: Answering Questions on the Prophetic

My Visits to the Galactic Council of Heaven

The Parables of Jesus Made Simple: Updated and Expanded Edition

Great Cloud of Witnesses Speak: Old and New

Walking under an Open Heaven

A Message from My Angel: Book 1

Interviews with the Two Witnesses: Enoch and Elijah Speak

Gaining Freedom from Sex Addictions: Breaking Free of Pornography and Prostitutes

Mary Magdalene Speaks from Heaven: A Divine Revelation

Princess Diana Speaks from Heaven: A Divine Revelation

How to Hear God's Voice: Keys to Conversational Two-Way Prayer

Apostle John Speaks from Heaven: A Divine Revelation

What I Believe

Great Cloud of Witnesses Speak: God's Generals

You can find my published books on my Amazon author page here: http://tinyurl.com/jq3h893

Upcoming Books

Christian Discipleship Made Simple

King David Speaks from Heaven: A Divine Revelation

About Matthew Robert Payne

Matthew was raised in a Baptist church and was led to the Lord at the tender age of eight. He has experienced some pain and darkness in his life, which has given him a deep compassion and love for all people.

Today, he's a founding member and admin of a Facebook group called "Prophetic Training Group," and he invites you to join him there. Matthew has a commission from the Lord to train up prophets and to mentor others in the Christian faith. He does this through his Facebook posts and by writing relevant books on the Christian faith.

God has commissioned him to write at least fifty books in his life, and he spends his days writing and earning the money to self-publish. You can support him by donating money at http://personal-prophecy-today.com or by requesting any of the other services available through his ministry website.

Recently, the Lord has put it on his heart to start his own publishing company called Christian Book Publishing USA. It is Matthew's hope to help other people self-publish their books in the future.

Matthew prays that this book has blessed you, and he hopes it will lead you into a deeper and more intimate relationship with God.

www.ingramcontent.com/pod-product-compliance
Lightning Source LLC
Chambersburg PA
CBHW052117070526
44584CB00017B/2528